THE PAPER AIRPLANE BOOK

Also by SEYMOUR SIMON

Science in a Vacant Lot
Chemistry in the Kitchen

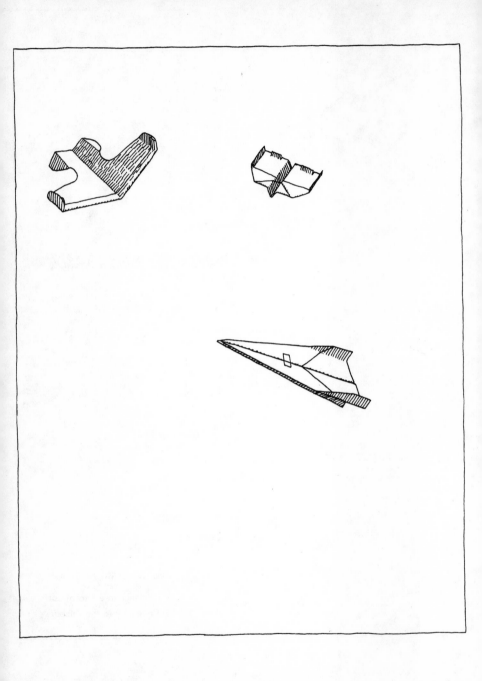

THE PAPER AIRPLANE BOOK

by SEYMOUR SIMON

ILLUSTRATED BY BYRON BARTON

THE VIKING PRESS

NEW YORK

FOR JOYCE,
WHO LOVES FLYING IN REAL AIRPLANES

Have you ever flown a paper airplane? Sometimes it twists and loops through the air and then comes to rest, soft as a feather. Other times a paper airplane climbs straight up, flips over, and dives headfirst into the ground.

What keeps a paper airplane in the air? How can you make a paper airplane go on a long flight? How can you make it loop or turn? Does flying a paper airplane on a windy day help it to stay aloft? What can you learn about real airplanes by making and flying paper airplanes? Let's experiment to discover some of the answers.

Take two sheets of the same-sized paper. Crumple one of the papers into a ball. Hold the crumpled paper and the flat paper high above your head. Drop them both at the same time. The force of gravity pulls them both downward. Which paper falls to the ground first? What seems to keep the flat sheet from falling quickly?

We live with air all around us. Our planet earth is surrounded by a layer of air called the atmosphere. The atmosphere extends hundreds of miles above the surface of the earth.

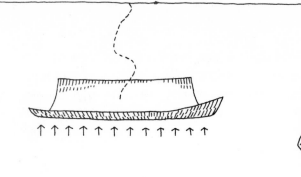

Air is a real substance even though you can't see it. A flat sheet of paper falling downward pushes against the air in its path. The air pushes back against the paper and slows its fall. A crumpled piece of paper has a smaller surface pushing against the air. The air doesn't push back as strongly as with the flat piece, and the ball of paper falls faster. The spread-out wings of a paper airplane keep it from falling quickly down to the ground. We say the wings give a plane *lift*.

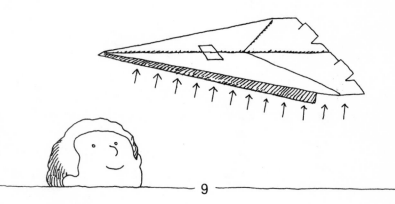

Here's how you can see and feel what happens when air pushes. Place a sheet of paper flat against the palm of your upturned hand. Turn your hand over and push down quickly. You can feel the air pressing against the paper. The paper stays in place against your palm. You can see the paper's edges pushed back by the air.

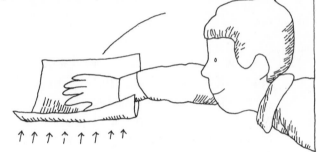

Now hold a piece of crumpled paper in your palm. Again turn your hand over and push down. The smaller surface of the paper hits less air. You feel less of a push against your hand. Unless you push down very quickly, the paper will fall to the ground before your hand reaches the ground.

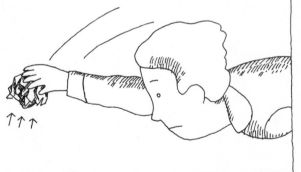

You want a paper airplane to do more than just fall slowly through the air. You want it to move forward. You make a paper airplane move forward by throwing it. Usually the harder you throw a paper airplane, the farther it will fly. The forward movement of an airplane is called *thrust*.

Thrust helps to give an airplane lift. Here's how. Hold one end of a sheet of paper and move it quickly through the air. The flat sheet hits against the air in its path. The air pushes up the free part of the moving paper. A paper airplane must move through the air so that it can stay up for longer flights.

Try moving the paper slowly through the air. Does the air push up the slow-moving paper as much as before? What do you think happens when a paper airplane stops moving forward through the air?

You can show that the same thing will happen if you run with a kite in the air. The air pushes against the tilted underside of the moving kite and lifts it up. What happens to the lift pushing up on the kite if you walk slowly rather than run?

The front edges of the wings of a real airplane are usually tilted slightly upward. As with a kite, the air pushes against the tilted underside of the wings, giving the plane lift. The greater the angle of the tilt the more wing surface the air pushes against. This results in a greater amount of lift. But

if the angle of the tilt is too great, the air pushes against the larger wing surface presented and slows down the forward movement of the plane. This is called *drag*.

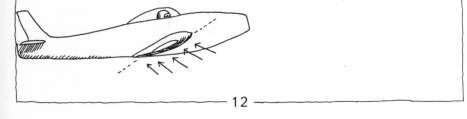

Drag works to slow a plane down, as *thrust* works to make it move forward. At the same time, *lift* works to make a plane go up, as *gravity* tries to make it fall down. These four forces are always working on paper airplanes just as they work on real airplanes.

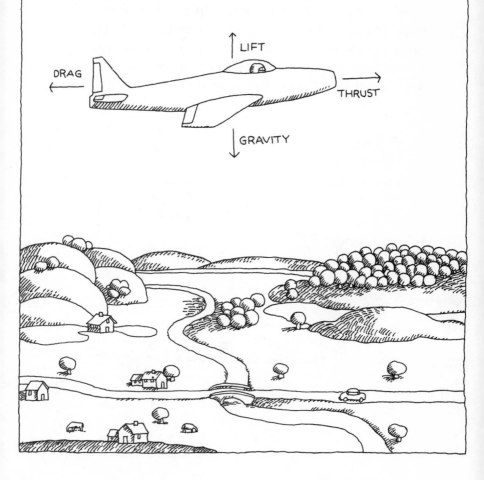

There is still another way most real airplanes and some paper airplanes use their wings to increase lift. The top side as well as the bottom side of the wing can help to give the plane lift.

The secret lies in the shape of the wing. The front edge of an airplane's wing is rounded and thicker than the rear edge. The top surface of the wing is curved while the bottom surface of the wing is almost straight. Look at the drawing. You can see that the distance across the top of the wing is greater than the distance across the bottom.

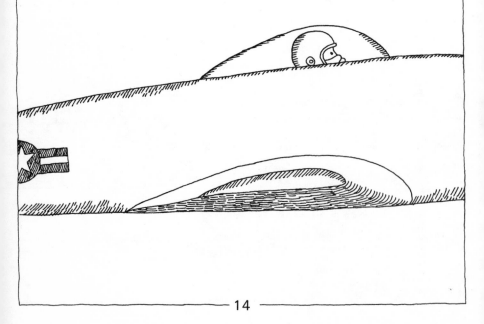

Thrust makes the airplane move through the air. The shape of the wing forces the air to move over and under it. The air moving over the top reaches the back of the wing at the same time as the air moving across the bottom of the wing. But the air crossing the top has farther to travel than the air crossing the bottom. So the air at the top must move faster than the air at the bottom.

The faster air moves, the less it presses sideways. The rapidly moving air atop the wing presses downward with less force than the air underneath the wing presses upward. This gives an airplane much of its lift.

Here's how you can show this. Bend a piece of stiff paper into a curve and rest it on a flat surface. Blow under the curve of the paper. Instead of lifting up, the paper will be pressed down. Can you explain why?

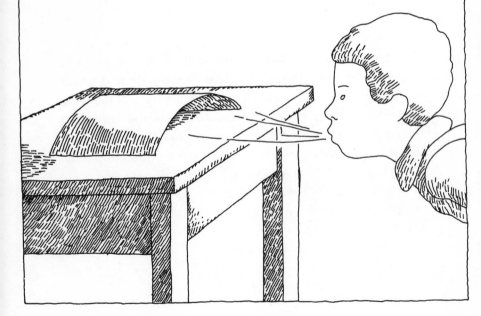

Here are some other ways to show the same principle. Hold two thin sheets of paper between your fingers so that they hang downward with a space between them. Blow between the papers. What do you think will happen? Why?

You can try the same thing with two ping-pong balls taped to threads. Hang them downward from the edge of a table and blow between them. Can you explain what happens?

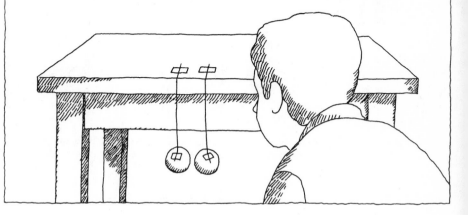

Let's make a paper airplane and see how these forces work in flight. Use a sheet of $8\frac{1}{2}$-by-11-inch paper. For this plane you can also use heavy art paper or construction paper.

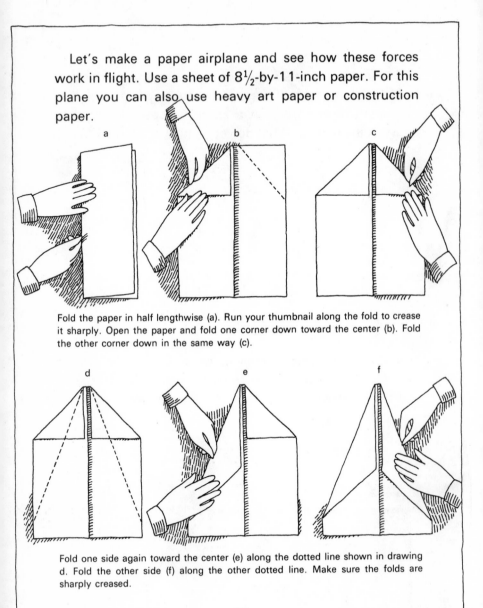

Fold the paper in half lengthwise (a). Run your thumbnail along the fold to crease it sharply. Open the paper and fold one corner down toward the center (b). Fold the other corner down in the same way (c).

Fold one side again toward the center (e) along the dotted line shown in drawing d. Fold the other side (f) along the other dotted line. Make sure the folds are sharply creased.

Turn the paper over. Fold one side over (h) along the left-hand dotted line shown in drawing g. Open the paper. Fold the other side over (i) along the right-hand dotted line in drawing g. From the bottom your plane should look like the one in drawing j.

UPWARD TILT

Use a piece of cellophane tape to hold the body of the plane together and to give the wings a slight upward tilt (k).

Launch your plane in a large room or out-of-doors. Make sure that there are no easily broken objects it can hit and knock over. Hold the fuselage of the plane between your thumb and forefinger a few inches back from its nose. Raise your hand high over your head and throw the plane gently forward. Throw the plane at a slight upward angle to the ground. If the plane climbs steeply and then dives into the ground, adjust the angle of thrust a bit downward. If the plane just dives into the ground, adjust the angle upward. Which angle of launch gives you the longest flights?

Try increasing the plane's thrust by throwing it harder. Does the plane fly longer or higher? Is it possible to throw the plane too hard? What happens then?

If your plane flutters and slips from side to side, try putting a paper clip on the body. The added weight of the clip helps the plane push through the air more easily and smoothly. Fasten the clip a bit closer to the front of the plane than to the back. If the plane climbs too sharply when you launch it, move the paper clip a little bit forward. If the plane dives without climbing, move the clip farther back. Find out what happens to the flight of your plane when you move the clip all the way forward or all the way back.

What happens if you hold the plane in launch position and then just drop it from a height? Does it fall directly, or glide down for a landing? How does the position of the paper clip affect the way the plane falls?

The position of the clip changes the point at which the plane's weight is balanced. This point is called the *center of gravity*. To find the center of gravity of your plane, place one finger under the front of the plane and another finger under the back of the plane. Move your fingers slowly in toward the center of the plane. The plane's center of gravity is where it balances on one finger.

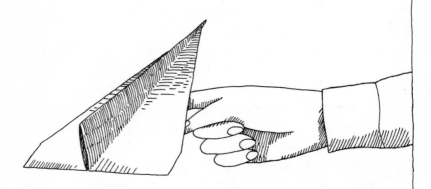

What happens to the position of the center of gravity when you add a paper clip? Where does the center of gravity have to be for the longest flights? Where is the center of gravity when the plane climbs steeply at launching? When it dives steeply at launching?

Adding a paper clip not only changes the plane's balance point but also adds to the plane's weight. Try flying the plane with two paper clips in the same position. Does the plane stay up in the air as long as it does with one clip? Try adding three paper clips. What happens now? What do you think would happen if you added ten paper clips? Try it. You can see why real airplanes are made of lightweight metals. Planes must also have the weight of their cargo carefully balanced before take-off.

Try flying your plane out-of-doors on a slightly windy day. What happens? Is there any way to stop the plane from tossing about wildly? Try adding some paper clips to increase the weight of your plane. Does the added weight make the plane's flight any steadier?

Throw the plane into the wind and then try throwing it with the wind. Compare the two flights. In which direction does the wind seem to give the plane more lift? Which way does the flight last longer? Real airplanes try to take off and land into the wind. Can you explain why?

Try making some slight changes in the design of your paper airplane. Fold your plane as before. With a pair of scissors, make two $\frac{1}{2}$-inch cuts (about $1\frac{1}{2}$ inches apart) in the back edge of each wing. Fold the paper between the cuts at a slight upward angle. This will form *flaps* on the back of each wing.

Launch the plane with the flaps at this upward angle. How do the flaps seem to change the way the plane flies? Fold the flaps flat again and compare how the plane flies without them.

Try flying the plane with the flaps folded at a slightly downward angle. How does this flight compare with the others?

The flaps change the direction of the flight. As the plane moves through the air, the flaps push against the air. With an equal force, the air pushes back against the flaps.

To see what happens, hold the plane between your thumb and forefinger at its balance point. Fold the flaps upward. With your fingers push against the flaps in the same direction as the air would move. The back end of the plane is pushed down by your finger (or by the air when the plane is flying). Like a seesaw, when the back end of the plane is pushed down, the front end of the plane comes up. The plane climbs.

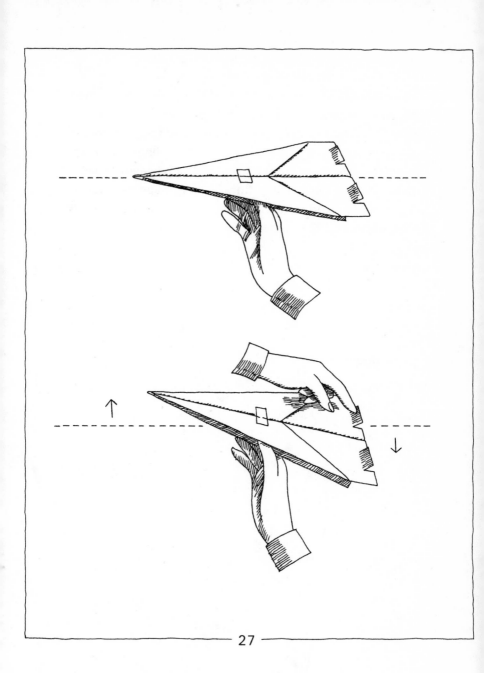

Fold the flaps downward and again push against them with your fingers. This time the back end of the plane is pushed up. The front end points down and the plane dives.

Change the angle at which you bend the flaps. Try flying the plane now. Does the angle of the flaps seem to make a difference in the plane's flight? Using flaps can add to the plane's lift. Add some paper clips to increase the weight of the plane and to see how the flaps help.

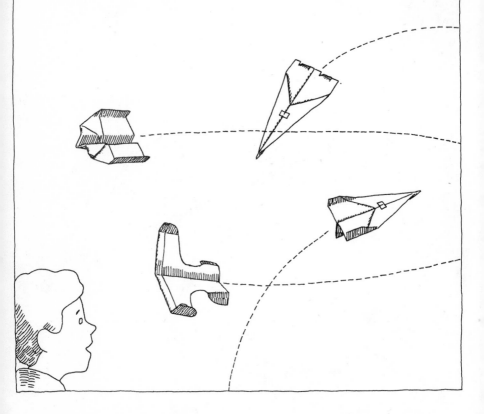

Fold one flap very slightly upward and the other flap very slightly downward. Fly the plane to see what effect the opposite-direction folds have. If the plane spins around, reduce the angle of the folds. Reverse the direction of the folds of each flap. Which way does the plane turn now? Try holding the plane at the balance point and pushing against the tilted flaps with your fingers to see why the plane turns.

What effect would increasing or decreasing the size of the flaps have? Try making the flaps longer or wider. If the flaps are very wide, the amount of drag increases greatly. What do you think will happen? Try it and see.

Most real airplanes have flaps on their wings and on the *horizontal stabilizers* in the tail of the plane. The flaps on the wings are used to increase the lift during take-offs and landings, when the plane is moving at its slowest speeds. Remember that the slower the plane moves through the air the less lift it gets. The pilot can vary the angle of the flaps to change the amount of lift.

The flaps in the back edge of the horizontal stabilizers are called *elevators*. Just like the flaps in the wing of a paper airplane, they make a real plane's nose point up—or down. This allows the pilot to reach the altitude he wants and to adjust this height during flight.

Set alongside the lift flaps on the wings of a real plane is another set of flaps called *ailerons*. These are tilted in opposite directions to make the plane roll to the right or to the left. How did you use the flaps on your paper airplane in these three different ways?

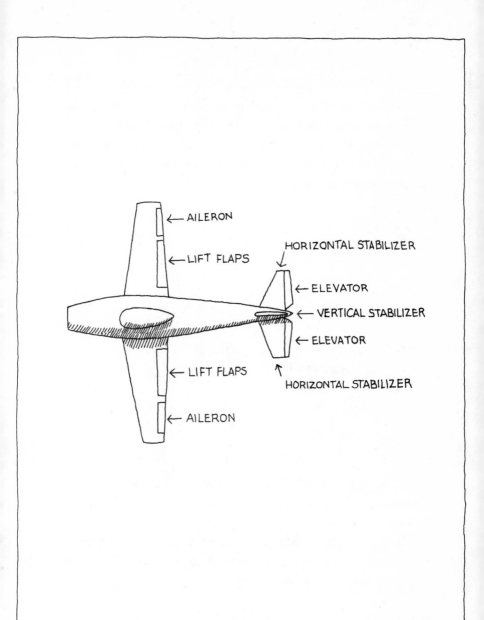

AILERON

LIFT FLAPS

HORIZONTAL STABILIZER

ELEVATOR

VERTICAL STABILIZER

ELEVATOR

LIFT FLAPS

HORIZONTAL STABILIZER

AILERON

To show how still another part of an airplane works, make the same model as you did before but without the flaps. This time, after you finish making the plane, fold the edges of the wings upward about one inch from the ends. The fold should be parallel to the plane's body and at right angles to the surface of the wings.

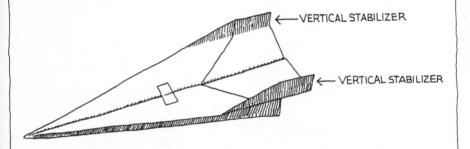

These right-angle folds act as *vertical stabilizers*. A vertical stabilizer makes a plane fly level and stops side-to-side swaying. The wings of your paper airplane act as horizontal stabilizers. These help to prevent bumpy, up-and-down movements. Fly your plane with and without the upward folds to see what effect they have on the flight. They will work best out-of-doors on a slightly windy day. Try bending the stabilizers downward instead of upward. In that direction, they may help your plane's lift as well as its stability. Try it and see.

Stabilizers work like the feathers on an arrow or the fins on the back of a dart. Cut a drinking straw down to a five-inch length. Throw it through the air as you would a dart. It will probably wobble from side to side or flip end over end.

Now cut four one-inch slits at right angles to each other.

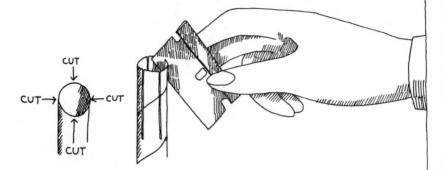

at one end of the straw. From some stiff paper such as an index card, cut out two 2-by-$\frac{1}{2}$-inch strips. Fold each strip in half lengthwise.

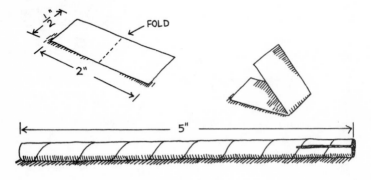

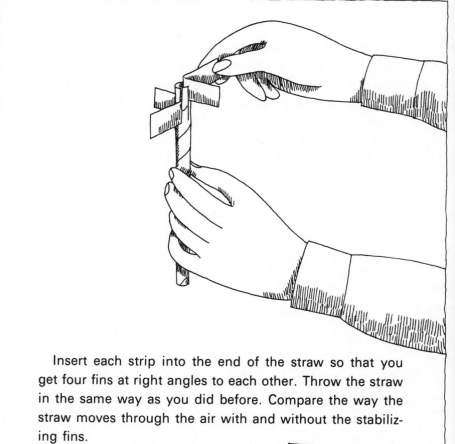

Insert each strip into the end of the straw so that you get four fins at right angles to each other. Throw the straw in the same way as you did before. Compare the way the straw moves through the air with and without the stabilizing fins.

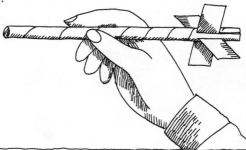

On your paper airplane you can use the back part of the vertical stabilizers to turn the plane left or right. Make a $\frac{1}{2}$-inch cut at the back of each stabilizer. Bend the folds slightly to the left. In which direction do you think the front of the plane will turn when in flight? Try it and see. Now bend the folds in the other direction. What happens now?

In a real plane there is usually one vertical stabilizer in the tail. The movable flap on the back edge of the stabilizer

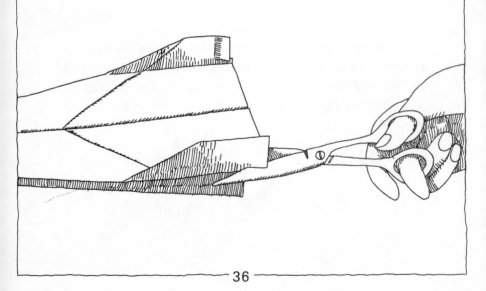

is called the *rudder*. The rudder works in a way similar to that of the elevators. When the rudder is angled to the left, it pushes against the air. The air pushes back and the tail of the plane swings to the right. When the tail of the plane moves right, the front of the plane moves left. Can you explain what happens when you angle a rudder to the right?

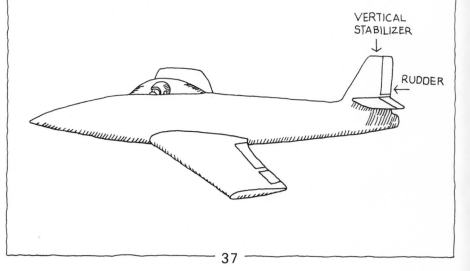

VERTICAL
STABILIZER

RUDDER

Experiment with other minor changes in the basic design of your paper airplane. For example, make the body very narrow so that the wings become very wide. Do you get more lift this way? What happens if you make the body wide and the wings narrow?

Try giving the wings a slight upward curve by gently rolling them over the edge of a table. Does this improve the flight time? What happens if you keep increasing the curve? Remember that while you increase the amount of lift by curving the wing, you also increase the amount of drag. Can you overcome the greater amount of drag by throwing the plane harder to give it more thrust?

Try making your plane with different weights of paper. Use lightweight onionskin, medium-weight typewriter paper, and heavyweight construction paper. Do they all fly equally well? Do some fly better with an easy throw and others with a harder throw? Try varying the angle at which you throw each plane.

If you can, launch a plane from a window or other high place. What kind of flight do you get? Which designs seem to glide better than others? Which stay up the longest? Do some models fly better in strong winds and others fly better without much wind? See if you can make slight changes which help to improve performance in each model.

Here's how to fold a blunt-nosed paper airplane that often stays up for long, looping flights. Use a sheet of $8\frac{1}{2}$-by-11-inch typing paper.

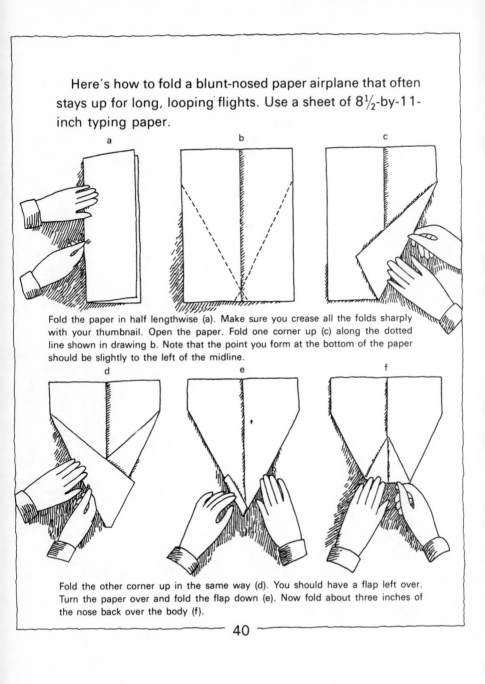

Fold the paper in half lengthwise (a). Make sure you crease all the folds sharply with your thumbnail. Open the paper. Fold one corner up (c) along the dotted line shown in drawing b. Note that the point you form at the bottom of the paper should be slightly to the left of the midline.

Fold the other corner up in the same way (d). You should have a flap left over. Turn the paper over and fold the flap down (e). Now fold about three inches of the nose back over the body (f).

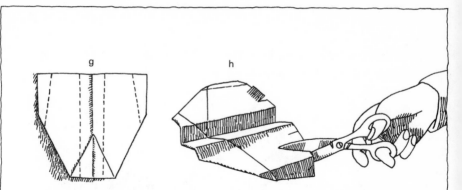

g

h

Refold the plane very firmly along the midline. Open the paper. Fold the left wing over along the dotted line shown to the left of the midline in drawing g. Fold the right wing over along the dotted line shown to the right of the midline in drawing g. Turn the plane over (h) and fold each wing tip down, along the dotted lines shown in drawing g. Cut small flaps in the back of each wing (h).

Start test-flying this model by folding both flaps upward. Launch from a high place or with a strong, forward push. The plane will probably loop around, glide, loop up, and glide again. You can get more loops by throwing the plane slightly upward and faster.

Try folding the flaps downward. Launch the plane with a slight upward throw. This time the plane will go into more of a gliding flight and come in for a smooth landing. This adjustment works quite well on a windy day. You will often get a smooth, long flight.

Try adjusting the angle of the flaps. Which one gives the most loops? Which one gives the longest flights? Also try making the plane with different kinds of paper, both light and heavy. Which weight seems to fly better indoors? Which flies better in the wind?

Here's how to make a plane that loops in an acrobatic way. Start with a piece of lightweight 8½-by-11-inch paper.

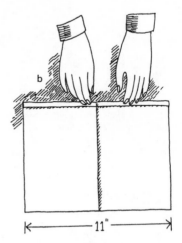

Fold the paper in half crosswise (a). Open the paper and make a crease along one of the long sides, ¼ inch from the edge (b). Make seven to ten more creases in the same way.

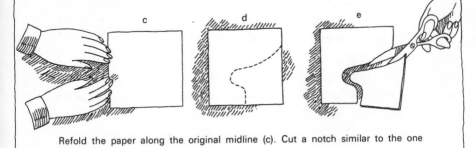

Refold the paper along the original midline (c). Cut a notch similar to the one shown (d and e).

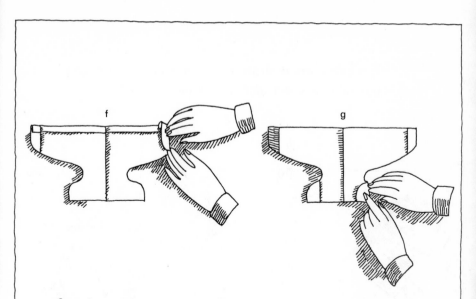

Open the paper and fold the tips of the wings up (f). Turn the paper over and fold the tips of the smaller rear wings down (g).

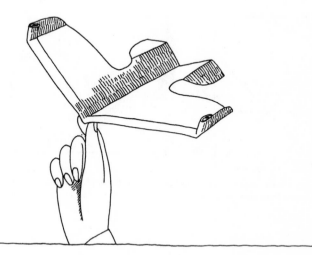

Another blunt-nosed airplane can be made in this way. Again start with a sheet of $8\frac{1}{2}$-by-11-inch paper.

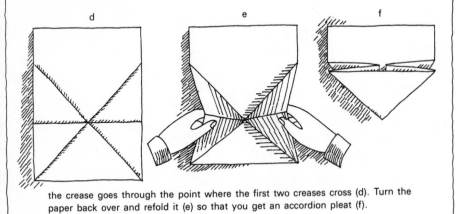

a   b   c

Holding the paper lengthwise, fold one corner up to the opposite side (a). Open the paper and fold the other corner up in the same way (b). Open the paper, turn it over, and fold the bottom up (c) so that

d   e   f

the crease goes through the point where the first two creases cross (d). Turn the paper back over and refold it (e) so that you get an accordion pleat (f).

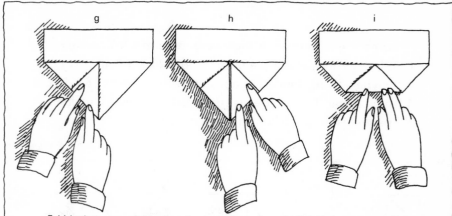

Fold both corners of the pleat down as shown (g and h). Fold the paper up (i) so that you get a blunt nose.

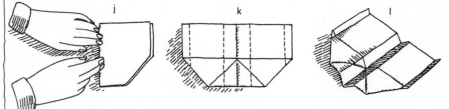

Fold the paper over along the midline (j), making a sharp crease, and reopen. Fold the left wing down along the dotted line shown to the left of the midline in drawing k. Fold the right wing down along the dotted line shown to the right of the midline in drawing k. Fold each wing tip up slightly along the dotted lines shown in drawing k (l).

Launch the plane with a strong, slightly upward push. The plane will fly in a straight line and give a very long flight. Make sure there is a lot of space in front of it.

To keep the plane in flight even longer, cut flaps in the back of each wing and bend them up slightly. There's nothing fancy about the way this plane flies. It just stays up for a long time. Try making it with a lighter-weight paper for even longer flights.

Some paper airplanes look very different from others. Here's how to make a plane that looks like a flying wing, or maybe a flying saucer. Again start with a sheet of $8\frac{1}{2}$-by-11-inch paper. Follow the instructions for making the plane on pages 44 and 45, up through step *h*.

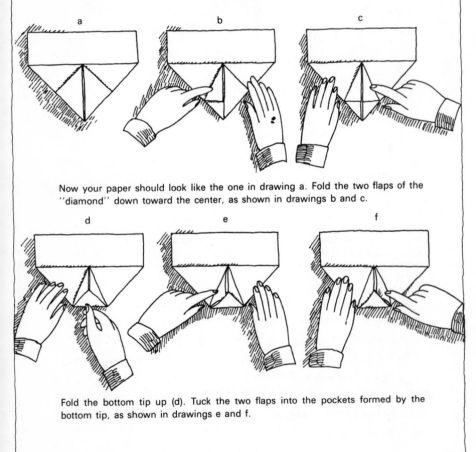

Now your paper should look like the one in drawing a. Fold the two flaps of the ''diamond'' down toward the center, as shown in drawings b and c.

Fold the bottom tip up (d). Tuck the two flaps into the pockets formed by the bottom tip, as shown in drawings e and f.

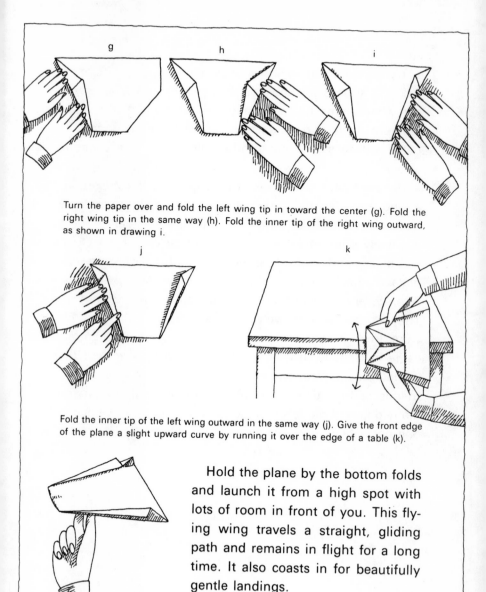

g   h   i

Turn the paper over and fold the left wing tip in toward the center (g). Fold the right wing tip in the same way (h). Fold the inner tip of the right wing outward, as shown in drawing i.

j   k

Fold the inner tip of the left wing outward in the same way (j). Give the front edge of the plane a slight upward curve by running it over the edge of a table (k).

Hold the plane by the bottom folds and launch it from a high spot with lots of room in front of you. This flying wing travels a straight, gliding path and remains in flight for a long time. It also coasts in for beautifully gentle landings.

Try designing and flying your own model paper airplanes. Ask your friends to show you their best designs. When you get what seems to be a good design, try throwing it in different ways and at different angles. Some models fly better with a strong push; others fly better with a gentle throw.

Use rear flaps with care. A little bend in the flaps goes a long way. Too much of a flap angle and the plane may crash. The same goes for curves in the wing. A gentle curve is usually more effective than a sharp curve.

Building and flying paper airplanes is fun for young people and adults too. Several years ago the well-known magazine, *Scientific American*, held a paper-airplane contest. They received almost twelve thousand entries. Many entries were from professors, engineers, and scientists. Entries came in from twenty-eight different countries around the world. Maybe you can hold a contest among your own friends or in your school. You might be surprised at the many different models entered. It seems as if almost everyone has a favorite paper airplane he likes to fly.